JUMP·ROPE

MUD PUDDLE BOOKS, INC.
New York, New York

Published by
Mud Puddle Books, Inc.
54 W. 21st Street, Suite 601
New York, NY 10010 USA

info@mudpuddlebooks.com

In association with
Hinkler Books Pty Ltd
17-23 Redwood Drive
Dingley Victoria 3172 Australia
www.hinklerbooks.com

© Hinkler Books Pty Ltd 2005

Written by: Chris Johnstone
Illustrated and designed by: JM Artworks

ISBN: 1-59412-087-0

Printed in China.

CONTENTS

INTRODUCTION

Children have been playing jump rope and chalk games for hundreds, even thousands, of years.

Both types of games are heaps of fun and great exercise outdoors in the fresh air.

Once you have mastered these games, you can even make up your own games! It is completely up to you and your imagination.

HISTORY - JUMP ROPE GAMES

Since the 1850s children have been playing jump rope games.
It started when a group of children were playing around with
a bunch of thin vines - I'm sure their parents told them not
to do this!

These vines were used as the first ever "jump ropes," even
though they were not as fancy or as colorful as the ones you
would find today.

The art of jump rope has come a long way since then. There are many fun games that you can play. Even boxers and athletes use jump ropes to keep fit.

Tip

When you are playing jump rope games, make sure that you play in an open area, so that your rope doesn't get caught on anything, or break anything.

JUMP ROPE WITH A SONG

This is one of the simplest jump rope games in the world. It's also lots of fun, and a great way to learn how to jump rope.

What you need

- two or more friends
- a long jump rope
- your loudest voices

What to do

Your friends need to swing the rope in a looping motion, either clockwise or counterclockwise. There should be a "sweet spot," where the rope is just slightly touching the ground as it swings around in the air.

When you are ready, jump into the sweet spot. This is more difficult than it sounds. You have to use good timing, so that the rope doesn't hit you when you jump in.

Once you have made it into the sweet spot, make sure that you jump every time the rope revolves around, otherwise the rope will catch around you and you are out.

Once you are out, it's time to let somebody else have a turn at jumping. You can have a go at turning the rope at one end.

Tip

To help make these games more interesting, you can also sing songs to the tempo of the jump rope. Here's an easy one to remember.

Jumping, jumping, all alone,
Can you make it on your own?
When you finish, there's no doubt
Pack your bags up, you are OUT.

Tip

If you are one of the rope turners, you can make the song quicker every time that you repeat it, until the person in the middle can't jump fast enough and is out.

CONTINUOUS JUMP ROPE

What you need
- as many friends as you can find
- a long jump rope
- your loudest singing voices
- an open area to jump rope in

What to do

Two of your friends need to hold the long jump rope at either end, and start turning the rope as they did in the first activity.

This time, you are going to have a whole group lining up, ready to jump into the sweet spot.

You need to take turns at jumping in the sweet spot. The first person starts jumping, and the rest of the group can sing the following song.

Once you've heard the line "It's over to you" it's time for you to jump out of the sweet spot, and for one of your friends to jump in. Then you can start it all over again.

I'm a little French kid

Dressed in gray.

Here are the things

I like to play:

Salute to the captain,

Bow to the queen,

Now go sailing

On a submarine.

I can do the tap dance,

I can do the splits,

I can do the Hokey Pokey

Just like this:

A Hokey Pokey one

A Hokey Pokey two

Now my friend,

It's over to you.

Now that you're used to it, you can jump to this song and do actions at the same time, while still jumping. Are you skilled enough to do both things at the one time? It does take a bit of practice.

Salute to the captain

I'm a little French kid
Dressed in gray.
Here are the things
I like to play:
Salute to the captain,

Bow to the queen

Bow to the queen,
Now go sailing
On a submarine.

I can do the tap dance

I can do the tap dance,
I can do the splits,
I can do the Hokey Pokey
Just like this:

TAP   TAP

I can do the Hokey Pokey

A Hokey Pokey one,
A Hokey Pokey two,
Now my friend,
It's over to you.

Tip

Don't worry about trying to do the full splits when you are jumping rope. Just do a "V" shape with your legs.

MOVING HOUSE

This next one is a fast one. The trick is to jump into the sweet spot one after the other.

What you need

- a long jump rope
- about five or more people
- an open area to jump rope in

What to do

Elect two people to be rope turners.

Once the rope is turning, get ready to jump into the sweet spot. As you are jumping, sing the following song.

When you hear the second line of the song, it is time for you to exit the sweet spot and let the next person in.

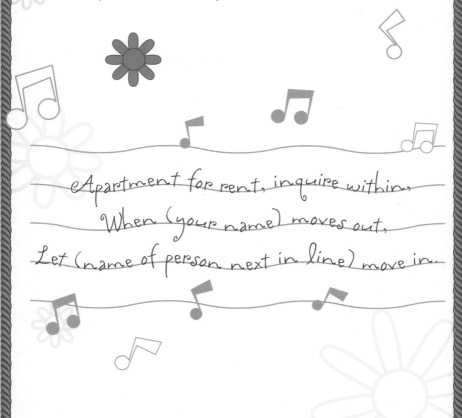

Apartment for rent, inquire within,
When (your name) moves out,
Let (name of person next in line) move in.

Here's an example of how the song would sound if the people playing were called Jason, Nicky, Norna, Chris and Josephine.

Apartment for rent, inquire within,
When **Jason** moves out, let **Nicky** move in.

Apartment for rent, inquire within,
When **Nicky** moves out, let **Norna** move in.

Apartment for rent, inquire within,
When **Norna** moves out, let **Chris** move in.

Apartment for rent, inquire within,
When **Chris** moves out, let **Josephine** move in.

Apartment for rent, inquire within,
When **Josephine** moves out, let **Jason** move in.

Keep going until somebody touches the rope or misses their turn.

Tip

If you want to, you can make the song and the rope turning go faster and faster until somebody is out.

DOGS AND CATS

What you need

- a long jump rope
- three friends
- an open area to jump rope in

What to do

Choose two of your friends to turn the rope, and the other two of you need to stand behind each of them.

Once the rope is in full swing, it's time to start playing.

To start the game, the two rope turners sing the following song.

Who is the fastest?
I don't know,
Come on Cat, come on Dog,
Time to gO!

Once you've heard the word "Go," you have to run clockwise, in a figure eight, through the swinging jump rope and around the rope turners.

Now you have to try to catch your friend and tag them on the back.

If you are tagged on the back or you touch the rope when you are running, you lose and become the Dog.

The Cat is the winner, and stays on to try to tag the next Dog.

The Dog becomes a rope turner and gives someone else a try at Dog and Cat.

Tip

It is really hard to run as fast as you can while taking time to jump or run under the rope. Quite often slow and steady will win the race.

JUMP ROPE RACES

Running races is a good way to exercise outside. This game is like a running race, except we aren't running, we're jumping rope! This can be heaps of fun for the whole family and can include as many people as you like. It is also a great way to practice jump rope.

What you need
- small (single person) jump ropes. You need one for each person playing.
- as many people as you can find
- a large open area, preferably on grass
- two balloons tied to weights, with string. The weights could be rocks or paper weights.

What to do

Find an area that is clear of obstacles and is suitable for a running race.

Decide where you want the race to start and finish. It is up to you how long you want the race to be.

Place one balloon, tied to its weight, at the point where you want to start the race. This will be your start and finish line.

Place the other balloon, tied to its weight, at a suitable distance from the start and finish line. This will be your halfway point

Arrange everybody behind the start and finish line.

START

FINISH

In your clearest, loudest voice, yell,

"READY, SET, GO!"

It is now a race between your friends. You have to jump rope, using your individual jump ropes, all the way from the start and finish line, across the ground until you reach the halfway point.

Then you must jump rope all the way around the halfway point and come back to the start and finish line. The first person to touch the balloon at the start and finish line is the winner.

FILL THE BOAT

What you need

- a large jump rope
- as many people as you can find
- a large open area suitable for jump rope

What to do

Two of your friends need to hold either end of the jump rope. Ask them to turn the rope as shown in the first activity.

Jump into the sweet spot. As you are jumping, sing the following song.

Sailing on my yacht today
Off to places far away
How many people, do you think?
Can we have until my yacht will sink?
One.

Once you have completed the song, it is time for the next person to jump in with you.

You sing the same song, but this time at the end you count

"One, two."

Now another person can jump in. Sing the song again but this time at the end of the song you count "one, two, three."

Keep following this pattern until you have as many people as you can, all jumping rope at the same time.

When somebody touches the rope, the boat is full. Then it is time to start again.

FOLLOW THE JUMPER

This game gives the jumper all the control. You choose where the rope turners have to walk, because they have to follow you.

What you need

- a jump rope
- at least two friends
- an open area to jump rope in

What to do

Choose two friends to be rope turners.

Stand in the sweet spot and start jumping rope.

When you are jumping, the rope turners can sing the following song.

Follow the jumper
Oh, so slow.
Where they'll end up
I don't know.

While you are jumping and singing, you must decide where you want to jump, and it is up to the rope turners to follow you to where you jump.

Once you have tripped up or touched the rope, it's time for one of the rope turners to have a turn at being the jumper.

Tip
This game requires a lot of concentration for all the players, even the rope turners!

Tip
When you are the jumper, try to roam far and wide. The results can be a lot of fun, and you may end up in some strange places.

JUMPING THE GAUNTLET

Now that you have improved your jump rope skills, this game will challenge you. It is a test of all your strength, coordination and stamina. Can you jump the gauntlet?

What you need
- three long jump ropes
- at least six friends
- an open area to jump rope in

What to do

Organize your six friends to be rope turners. Have two at each end of the three jump ropes.

Ask the rope turners to line up side by side, with about 10 feet (3 meters) between each jump rope.

It's now time for the rope turners to start turning their ropes. As they do this, they sing the following chant.

Can you jump the gauntlet?
Is it yes or no?
On your marks,
Now get set,
And go, go, go!

Now it's up to you. You have to jump through all of the jump ropes and back without tripping or touching the ropes, as fast as you can. This can be extremely tricky.

Once you have completed the gauntlet, or have touched the rope, it is time for someone else to have a turn.

If you are finding it too easy to play, you can ask the rope turners to turn the ropes faster.

Tip
If you really want to make this game into a competition, you can have somebody use a stopwatch to time how fast each of you can jump the gauntlet. Whoever has the fastest time wins!

CATERPILLAR

This is a game where there will be 3 winners.

What you need

- a long jump rope
- lots of people, as many as you can find
- an open area to jump rope in

What to do

Elect two of your friends to be rope turners at either side of the long rope.

The rest of you can line up in front of the jump rope.

Once the rope is turning, jump into the sweet spot and then exit on the other side of the rope.

As you are exiting, the next jumper enters the sweet spot and does the same.

Everyone in the line does this. If they touch the rope, or are too slow and allow the rope to turn before entering, they are out.

Once everybody in the line has gone through or is out, it is time for you to enter the sweet spot from the opposite side, following the same pattern.

The last three people left are the winners.

Tip This game becomes harder when more people are eliminated, as it is difficult to keep up the pace. Towards the end of the game, you have to be very quick to stay in.

JUMP LIKE ME!

This game is not a competition - it is just heaps and heaps of fun.

What you need
- a long jump rope
- a group of friends
- a wild imagination

What to do

Elect two of your friends to be rope turners and ask them to start turning the rope.

Assemble the rest of the group in a line, ready to jump into the sweet spot.

The first person to jump sings the following little poem.

Come on everybody, now, jump like me,
After my go, I want you to be . . .

Before you jump in, you have to say what you want the next person to be, for example, a monkey.

Then you have to do your best monkey jump rope actions.

After you have monkeyed around for a while, exit the sweet spot and let the next person be a monkey, until everyone in the line has had a go.

"monkey"

It's now someone else's turn to think up a crazy animal or person with crazy actions for everybody to do. You could be:

- a giraffe
- an astronaut
- an airplane
- a soldier

an astronaut

an airplane

a soldier

Tip You can do actions for any kind of thing that you want - it's up to you.

FASTER, FASTER, FASTER!

Remember, in all these games, you can build up the speed of the rope being turned, to make it even more difficult – and to really test people out.

One way of doing this is to cry out words that explain how fast to go. There are several ways of doing this, but the most common is "Salt, Pepper, Vinegar."

"Salt, Pepper, Vinegar."

Salt – fast
Pepper – faster
Vinegar – really fast, almost impossible to keep up with

How high?

You can vary the height of the rope, by calling out "higher" and turning the rope in a big, high loop.

You can also call out "lower," turning the rope in a much flatter, lower loop.

HISTORY - CHALK GAMES

One of the most famous chalk games of all time is called hopscotch. It was invented by the ancient Romans about three thousand years ago.

Initially hopscotch was used as a way of training their soldiers. It helped them with their balance and footwork.

Since then chalk games have been played by children (and adults) all over the world.

CHALK FACTS

Chalk is a repellent to snails, slugs, and ants. These creepy-crawlies will never cross a chalk line.

You can use chalk to absorb oil and grease.

Many fantastic artists use chalk to draw on pavements. These masterpieces only last until the next time it rains, or when a street sweeper rolls over it.

Chalk is used in lots of different sports to mark the lines on the ground. It is also used in:
- weightlifting – it is ground into a powder and rubbed on the contestants' hands. This absorbs the moisture to stop the weights from slipping from people's hands.
- snooker, pool, and billiards – a bit of chalk at the end of the cue stick helps control the white ball.

Tip

When you are playing chalk games, make sure that you play them outside, on a surface that is easy to draw on.

MAGIC SNAIL

What you need
- an open area of concrete, that you are allowed to draw on with chalk
- chalk
- lots of people

What to do

Draw a large spiral (shaped like a snail's shell) on the ground. Make a circle in the center and label it "home."

Divide the rest of the spiral into thirteen spaces.

Label the space furthest from home as "start."

To start, you must hop on one foot, landing in each space, all the way from the start space to the home circle.

You can land on both feet in the home circle before turning and hopping back out.

If you complete the feat without stepping on a line, you can write your initials in the space of your choice. No other player can land there for the rest of the game.

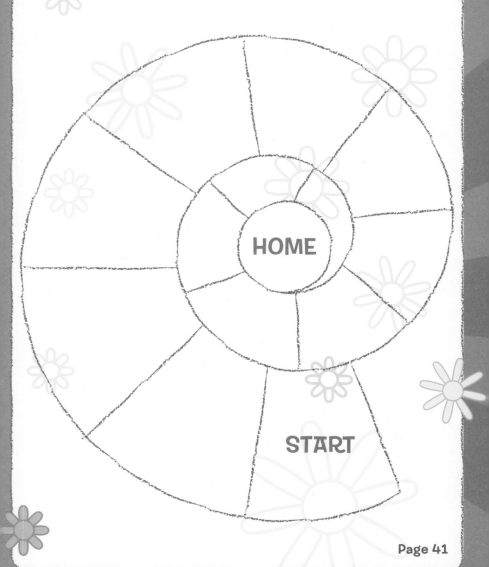

HOME

START

The next person in line then tries their luck at hopping to and from the center, remembering to jump over the initialed block.

If they succeed, they earn a square, and are able to initial it.

If a player can't make it to home, they can't initial any spaces, and must wait until it's their turn again.

Play continues in this manner until no one is able to reach home.

Whoever has earned the most spaces wins.

HOME

START

Tip

It doesn't really matter if you win or lose. What really matters is that you are exercising outside and having fun with your friends.

NOUGHTS, CROSSES, AND STONES

What you need
- an open area of concrete, that you are allowed to draw on with chalk
- chalk
- at least two stones
- a playing partner

What to do

Draw a large box on the pavement and a tic tac toe (naughts and crosses) grid inside it.

You start by trying to toss a stone into one of the squares. If you succeed, you can mark the space with an X.
A marker that lands on any of the lines is considered a miss.
Then, the other player tries to earn a square, marking their win with an O.

The first to fill three squares in a row wins.

Tip

You can make this game trickier by standing further and further away from the square when you are throwing the stones.

PEOPLE OUTLINE PICTURES

This game is one of the funniest and most creative chalk games you can play. Do you know why? Because there are no winners or losers – it's just lots and lots of fun.

What you need

- an open area of concrete, that you are allowed to draw on with chalk
- colored chalk
- a partner

What to do

Ask your friend to lie down on the ground, on their back. Make sure there are no stones or leaves on the ground, as this will make it uncomfortable to lie down.

Draw an outline of your friend as they lie down on the ground.

Now your friend can stand up. You should be able to see your friend's body shape on the ground.

Now it's your turn to lie down and let your friend outline you.

Now that you can see both outlines, it's time to start work.

You can both fill in the spaces of the outlines, using the colored chalk. Try to make it look like your friend.

Once you have finished, you can stand back and admire your artwork.

Tip

You can lie down in different poses for more interesting outlines.

Tip

Use your imagination and fill in the outlines so that they look like different people or animals.

For example:

- a weightlifter
- a crossing guard
- a cheerleader
- a gorilla
- a space alien

You can do as many different pictures as you can imagine. It is up to you !

HOPSCOTCH

This is one of the oldest and most famous chalk games of all time. You can carry on this tradition by playing it.

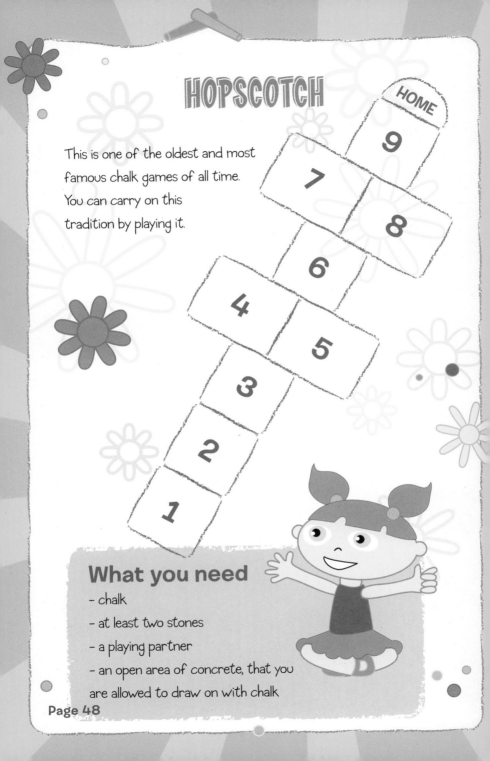

HOME

9

7

8

6

4

5

3

2

1

What you need
- chalk
- at least two stones
- a playing partner
- an open area of concrete, that you are allowed to draw on with chalk

What to do

This bit is a little tricky. Copy this diagram in the book on the ground, using your chalk. Make it quite big, about 10 feet (3 meters) long and about 3 feet (1 meter) wide. Use whatever color chalk you like.

Now it's time to play. Standing at the front of the grid, throw a stone as best as you can into the square marked "one."

If you do this successfully, you now have to hop over square one, and hop all the way to home, making sure that you hop once in each square on the way there and back.

You can land in the home square on two feet, and turn around in one jump, landing on two feet, before hopping back to the front of the grid.

You have to pick up your stone in square one on your way back, remembering to stay on one foot.

If you managed to stay on one foot the whole time, and didn't step on any lines, you can go to the front of the grid and try to throw the stone into the square marked "two."

Keep doing this until you make it through all the numbers and home, and do the same on the way back.

If you step on a line or throw your stone into the wrong square, it is the next person's turn.

The first person to be able to make it all the way up and back the grid is the winner.

Tip

There are different rules that you can add to this game if you want to. You can:

- mark your initials inside each box that you landed your stone on first, so only you can hop on it. This rule makes the game similar to Magic Snail.
- hop on your left foot on the way to home, and hop on your right foot on the way back.
- count the numbers aloud as you are hopping on them.

If there are any crazy rules that you think might work, give them a try.

4

3

TD

2

1

FOUR SQUARE

This is a splendid game that can last many hours and can involve as many people as you like. It is great exercise.

Ball

| K | 1 |
| 2 | 3 |

What you need

- chalk
- a tennis ball
- at least four people
- a big ruler
- an open area of concrete that you are allowed to draw on with chalk

What to do

Draw the four square diagram on a flat surface of concrete. It is up to you how big you want the court to be, but about 13 square feet (4 square meters) is a good starting point.

To make sure the lines are straight, use a big ruler.

Assemble yourself and three of your friends to stand in the four squares. Because it is your game, you can stand in the "K" square, which stands for king.

To start the game, as the king, you must serve the ball by bouncing it in your square once and then hitting it towards one of the other squares with your hand.

The receiving player then hits the ball to any other player, making sure it bounces once in their own square.

You can lose the point if you:
- hit the ball (or are hit by the ball) before it bounces once in your square
- do not hit the ball before it bounces twice
- hit the ball out of bounds (it must land in someone's square first)
- miss the ball completely or make a mistake

Once a point has finished, whoever lost the point has to go out. Whoever was behind that player in rankings takes their place.

For example:

If the person in square number three is out, the person in square number two goes to three. The person in square number one goes to two, and a new person goes to square one.

The person who is out must now wait in line until it is their turn to be in square one again.

It is the aim of the game to move to king status and stay there for as long as possible.

Remember to play fair and have fun.

Tip
If you have the room you can play six square, eight square or even ten square. If you're having a big family gathering you could play twenty-six square if you feel like it!

WORD-HOUSE OF MYSTERY

This is a great outside game that involves more thought than sport. You may even learn some new words.

What you need
- chalk
- an open area of concrete that you are allowed to draw on with chalk, or a blackboard
- another person to play with

What to do

Think of a word, but don't tell the other person what it is.

Write down, on the ground, a blank line for every letter that is in your word. For example, if your word has eight letters in it, draw eight lines.

The other player now has to guess letters that he or she thinks are in the word. If the person guesses correctly, write the letter in the appropriate space.

If the person guesses incorrectly, you can draw one line of this drawing.

If the other player guesses all the letters in the word before you have drawn the word-house of mystery, they win. If the word-house of mystery drawing is completed before they have guessed all the letters in the word, you win.

Tip You can take turns being the chooser and the guesser. You can even have different categories, such as:
- movie stars
- animals
- songs
- countries
- food

Tip It doesn't have to be a single word. You can use as many words as you like.

Tip If you're finding that the house is being built too quickly, you can make your house have a window, a chimney, or even a smiling sun in the background.

HAND TENNIS

This is an extremely popular schoolyard game. It is a lot of fun and very good exercise.

What you need
- a tennis ball
- chalk
- a playing partner
- a brick or concrete wall that you are allowed to draw on with chalk, and are allowed to throw a tennis ball against

What to do

With your chalk, draw a square on the ground ending at the wall, like the following diagram. This will be your playing court. You can make the playing court as big or small as you like.

With your chalk, draw a line across the wall. This will be your net. You can make the net as high or low as you want it to be.

Now it's time to play. You serve by throwing the tennis ball so that it bounces on the ground and then hits the wall over the net.

Once the ball has bounced off the wall and landed in the court, the other player has to hit the ball with their hands. As with the serve, you have to make sure the ball bounces on the ground before hitting the wall above the net, before landing in the court.

Keep playing like this until somebody loses a point.

You can lose a point by:
- hitting or serving the ball under the net
- hitting or serving the ball out of the court once it has hit the wall
- hitting the ball twice
- being unable to hit the ball when it is your turn

If you win a point, you can draw a mark on the wall, using your chalk.

Take turns in serving every point that is played.

The first player to win eleven points wins the game.

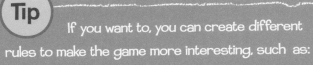

Tip

If you want to, you can create different rules to make the game more interesting, such as:

- only being able to play left-handed
- playing first to twenty-one points
- drawing a smiley face on the wall - you lose a point if you hit it with the tennis ball
- doubles - that means you have two teams of two people playing each other

The main point is to have fun!

LEARNING MORE

There are many different jump rope and chalk games out there. All you have to do is go out and find them. To do this you can use:

The Internet

Try typing "jump rope" or "chalk" into a search engine, and you'll be amazed at the amount of web sites devoted to them.

Your local library

There are heaps of books written about jump rope and chalk games. If you are having trouble finding them, ask the librarian to help you out.

PRACTICE, PRACTICE, PRACTICE

The only way to become better at something is to practice as much as you can. Practicing these games is not only fun, but it can be quite rewarding when you realize that you are improving all the time. So go out there and start practicing today!